ALCOHOLISM

Its Cause and Cure from the
Viewpoint of
Science of Mind

by
Ernest Holmes

Martino Publishing
Mansfield Centre, CT
2010

Martino Publishing
P.O. Box 373,
Mansfield Centre, CT 06250 USA

www.martinopublishing.com

ISBN 1-57898-922-1

© 2010 Martino Publishing

Cover design by T. Matarazzo

Printed in the United States of America On 100% Acid-Free Paper

ALCOHOLISM

Its Cause and Cure from the
Viewpoint of
Science of Mind

by

Ernest Holmes

Science of Mind
Los Angeles, CA
1941

Alcoholism

Its Cause and Cure from the Viewpoint of

Science of Mind

by

Ernest Holmes

By and large, alcoholic addiction is the result of a wrong adjustment to life; it is the result of an emotional unbalance, following one's inability squarely to meet the situations and conditions that arise in his personal experience. This inability to meet situations is, of course, largely unconscious;

that is, it is subjective, hidden, and therefore unknown to the conscious faculties.

When this maladjustment to life reaches a point where one becomes an habitual drunkard, it is evident that in an unconscious manner he is seeking self-destruction! His attempt to avoid the realities of his everyday contact with life has reached a point where delusion alone can compensate his imagination for that which he desires to become or to attain. Unconsciously, he seeks oblivion through self-destruction. Of course, the mental process whereby he arrives at this conclusion is mostly subjective.

We are all familiar with the type of person who, at a critical point in his career, gets drunk; the one who throws his finest opportunity to the wind and seeks oblivion through the loss of consciousness. At the moment that faith is needed, fear dominates. The desire to lose oneself, even to destroy oneself, becomes stronger than the assurance that he may meet and handle any situation that arises.

This does not mean, however, that everyone who drinks is seeking self-destruction. We are talking about that class of drinker who becomes submerged in the habit, and unfortunately, all too many drinkers of hard liquor are of this type. It is for those who suffer from an irresistible desire to become submerged in the habit that this article is written.

In such cases the habit, itself, is not the real disease. It is an unconscious attempt to escape from the real disease. The disease itself is some inner emotional state, of which the patient generally is not at all aware, but from which he *unconsciously* shrinks. He is impelled to seek escape through the act of self-forgetting or self-destruction. If this is the case, it follows that *the habit will be healed only when its cause is destroyed.* In other words, it is not *alcoholism*, as though it were a thing in itself, that should be attacked but the hidden cause back of the addiction that needs to be eradicated.

If the cure is to become a real and lasting healing, it will be accomplished only by first uprooting those hidden and subjective causes which lie back of the actual disease; the elimination of unconscious frustrations, whether they occurred in early youth or in later life; for addiction is an unconscious attempt either to express what is felt but not consciously known—to escape from some subjective restriction—or else, but self-destruction, to reach an imaginary oblivion.

This requires mental surgery, an expression which a few years ago might have caused amusement but which today is quite familiar among psychologists as well as among mental and spiritual practitioners. Indeed, mental surgery is a reality in many cases, and the things that may be operated upon mentally with hope of success, outnumber those that may be operated upon physically with the same expectation.

The alcoholic is not necessarily a mental, spiritual or moral weakling. Indeed, many of the best minds have experienced the flight into delusion, an unconscious attempt to escape from the real disease which is hidden.

Of course, there are other causes for certain forms of alcoholism: the often-indulged-in habit of the "pick me up," the bracer after a hard days work; the social habit of the too occasional cocktail, the environment of childhood, the tendency to form habits that others have, for fear of being thought queer or "sissy." Unfortunately, there are those who think that to be a good drinker of hard liquor is to be manly and virile. Nothing can be further removed from the truth. Often virility lies in abstinence, rather than in indulgence.

It is because the reasons for inebriety may be legion that the analyst finds such difficulty in uncovering them; perhaps a frustration in childhood, perhaps a faulty environment, possibly the result of a social habit, neglect and loneliness in childhood; a too indulgent father or mother, a desire to still remain at the mother's breast or under the father's guidance—a not-grown-up attitude—but in most cases of over-indulgence, some subtle inferiority complex is indicated.

Such flights into the unconscious generally are attempts to turn back the stream of life action into channels where there is no longer any self-discipline or self-restraint...such a lack of self-confidence that one feels he must have release from the real issues and problems of living. Thus we see that the cause of most alcoholism is the seed of desire planted in the garden of emotional unfulfillment; this produces a maladjustment to life and living. It follows, then, that to remove this inner conflict is also to remove its objective effect. And what is this but a healing of thought?

In the science of psychology this is accomplished by bringing the compulsion to the surface to be self-seen, and thereby dissipated. This is the *mental surgery* of psychology; the analysis of the soul, the taking apart and again reassembling of the psyche. The afflicted person has lost conscious demand of himself. His mental faculties have weakened. His physical, mental, emotional and spiritual faculties are no longer in proper balance. He is unstable and can no longer meet the everyday issues of life. He seeks flight into a world of fantasy and delusion, and, in extreme cases, it is believed by some that he seeks complete self-destruction. At any rate, he seeks to avoid whet he no longer feels competent to meet.

In turning from reality, the sufferer seeks the unreality of illusion. He temporarily feels himself supreme, the master of his destiny through fantasy rather than accomplishment. He is the "make believe" person, the overgrown child impersonating his desires through a make-believe world of delusion. In trying to express himself, he is never himself!

The form which any individual habit takes is naturally conditioned by the temperament of the one seeking self-expression. *There is really no single type of drinker.* The cause of overindulgence depends largely on the conditions surrounding the one who is afflicted with the habit, and as we are all individuals, so the cause must be handled in such a manner as to meet the individual need. This problem is always individual, as are all other problems. But there is a general theory underlying all such causes, and this theory (now accepted by most psychologists and mental practitioners) is that behind any habit where the one afflicted seeks escape from reality—that is from the normal contact with everyday life and its problems—there is a lack of true self-confidence; a dearth of self-realization; a lack of poise and balance.

This is shown by the fact that in nearly all such cases the patient is penitent, remorseful, discouraged, unhappy, nervous, irritable, dodges responsibility and is filled with self-condemnation. He fells himself "no good," not at all worthwhile, he is desperate and as soon as possible must seek flight again into his dream world—into his world of illusion where he reigns supreme in his own imagination. He is now king, creator, conqueror, the master of his own destiny. He feels confident, happy and, temporarily, self-sufficient. But alas, he is too soon deprived of his fleeting dream; the vision vanishes and the hard facts of reality again confront him with the life he must live. After each flight into illusion, he is less able to cope with the world of reality. More and more frequently he seeks his dream world, and finally he will do anything in his power to accomplish his purpose, which is to escape into the wilderness of self-deception.

And what of the cure, for cure there must be to every human ill?

The patient must be given back to himself, and there are two ways or methods through which this giving-back process may be accomplished.

The first way we shall mention is the field of psychology, unrelated to spiritual values, but none the less scientific. The patient is helped to see for himself where the real cause of his trouble lies. He must start with a real and a sincere desire to be healed; he must wish to be rid of his habit.

The psychologist is going to give the patient back to himself, and in the new life which the patient is to vision, alcohol plays and important part whatsoever. The subtle cause of the habit, which lies deep in the unconscious is to be uncovered and self-seen. This calls for the most complete cooperation between patient and psychologist.

The psychologist is understanding, patient and gentle, but he remorselessly probes into the lower streams of consciousness until he uncovers the cause of the disease. It has been discovered that *will* plays a minor role in this performance, while *imagination* plays a very important one indeed. In this system and procedure, it necessarily follows that the entire past of the patient must be "uncovered" and brought to light, that is, it must be self-seen, for self-seen it is self-dissipated. Naturally, such a process is cumbersome, long continued, and expensive. It could not be otherwise. The criticism often aimed at the psychologist because of the length of time it takes to make a complete analysis and because of the expense attached to the process, is generally unjustified. It is based on an entire ignorance of the principles involved.

It is evident that if a psychologist must uncover the facts of one's entire human experience, he cannot be expected to do so in a few days, weeks, or even months. And it is only fair to expect the psychologist to be adequately compensated for his time and effort. If more were known about the necessary and lengthy process of this treatment, less criticism would be leveled at those who devote their time and attention to its technique.

A complete analysis had taken place only when the whole story had risen to the surface: the early frustrations, the disappointments in childhood, the shocks of life, the dreams of daytime and evening, the fantasy of nighttime and the longings of waking hours—all of these must be taken into account. The shames, disillusionments, ambitions, hopes, fears and failures of an entire lifetime of self-experience are not quickly brought to the light of day. And the psychologist must at all times gently lead the patient to do the uncovering for himself. The psychologist directs and guides but does not do the talking himself.

In uncovering the inner life of his patient, the psychologist is exposing the entire field of emotional reaction; he is, as it were, sinking a shaft into the unconscious and bringing up, through he probing, bucket after bucketful of past experiences—some good, some bad, some indifferent—but the analysis is not complete until the last bucketful has been brought to the light of day, which means to the attention of the conscious thought.

The generalized term of "libido" is used to designate the field of emotion and emotional response to life and to living. The hidden forces of life which seek self-expression, the sum total of all desire, the life force itself, is what is meant by "the libido." These life forces seek self-expression and when turned back upon themselves through repression they, to use the words of Jung, "fester like arrows in our flesh." Again Jung says that "they psychoanalytic cure ... is understanding."

This emotional craving for self-expression starts at the mother's breast and continues throughout life. Frustrations, then, may be of an early date in the experience of the patient, and all experiences must be taken into account if the analysis is to be complete. In fact, its effectiveness depends upon its completeness. It is only reasonable to suppose that, for the average individual, such treatment is simply out of the question. In the first place, there would not be enough analysists enough to handle all the cases needing attention; and if there were, the process being so expensive, but few could take the advantage of it. This is self-evident and is already recognized by many leaders of the profession. What, then, is to become of the majority of cases who are unable to avail themselves of what is certainly a scientific and a most effective form of treatment?

It is to answer this question that this article is written. In spiritual science we believe that there is a Mind Principle which is ever present. It is responsive to all demands made upon it, responding alike to each and to all. The knowledge that this power of Mind is a reign of law, available for all purposes, is a dividing line between superstition and fear on the one hand, and science and intelligence on the other.

Like the psychologist, we believe that the issues of life are from within and not from without. Life surges into expression from some invisible, subterranean channel in the depths of our own being, "behold, the kingdom of god is within!"

As we pass from the visible to the invisible, we find finer and more illusive powers at work. The mineral world seems fixed, while in the animal and vegetable world there is constant flux and change. In the ether, we find light, heat and energy. Each plane or realm becomes finer as we pass from the visible to the invisible.

Some inner action in the ether, which acts like Mind or Intelligence, starts a series of vibrations in this medium, which, in its turn, induces a corresponding vibration in the more gross or less molecular substance, until mechanical action is produced. The invisible contains the final impulse for this energy; and everything proceeds from this invisible into visible form.

The most powerful forces operating in and through man are likewise invisible. This is why emotion has such power; why imagination may take form and become objectified in experience. Now the only way that spiritual forces can operate for us is through the avenues of thought action. This is why thought action is creative, actually molding conditions from invisible (but real) causes. The world of causes is in Mind and Spirit; the world of effects is in conditions and things. Since the Spirit is never evil, it follows that it is the use we make of the Life Principle which decides whether or not our lives shall be destructive or constructive.

The emotional craving for self-expression is not evil, and any belief that we must remove all desire before we can become spiritual, is just so much nonsense. If we could remove all desire for self-expression, then we should no longer exist. An attempt to remove all desire is an unconscious impulsion toward self-oblivion, which arises from a maladjustment to life.

All outward self-expression is the product of thought, whether or not the thought be conscious, for unconscious thought is thought action just as truly as is conscious thought.

Mental and emotional experiences are activities of the intelligence that is within us. The multiplication if ideas or the subtraction of ideas from the mental are actual activities. Where there are a given number of thought impulses, there will be a corresponding physical reaction. Wherever there is a different arrangement of thought, there will be a corresponding and a new reaction to life and to living. This is the secret of analytical psychology. The probing, the purging, the cleansing process of thought, which takes place as undesirable thought impulses are removed and transmuted or sublimated into other channels.

The re-education of the psyche, the re-orientation of the intellect, the re-integration of the personality, is but the giving back to the individual that which he has never really lost but that which, through a new and better understanding of himself, he now uses in a constructive way. The analyst has nothing whatsoever to give; he may only reveal. He has nothing to add to or take from; he may only rearrange.

The analyst must reveal the patient to himself. It is the truth known to his conscious mind that sets him free. "...And ye shall know the truth and the truth shall make you free."

It is wonderful to realize that we are complete within ourselves, *even when we seem so incomplete*. This is the basis upon which soul analysis may hope to become permanently successful. Jung has definitely stated that there can be no permanent cure of a neurosis without a restoration of confidence and faith. I have known many other scientific workers in the same field who have made similar statements. It seems self-evident that this must be true.

But just how does the method of spiritual mind healing compare with the methods of psychology? This question is put with no thought of belittling the methods of psychology, which are recognized as scientific, constructive and effective. The question is put merely to answer the need of the larger number of sufferers who have neither the time nor the financial means necessary to follow the more cumbersome method.

Like the psychologist, the mental and spiritual practitioner recognized that the seat of the trouble lies in the unconscious realm of desire and unfulfillment. He knows that people actually hunger and thirst after self-expression. He also knows that when people "hunger and thirst after righteousness" they will be filled. After *righteousness*, means after a constructive mode of living. The psychologist starts with the assumption that the patient must be given back to himself. But how could he be given back to himself, unless there were first a real Self to be given back to? As a matter of fact, the psychologist really does uncover the *self* to the patient's mental eye. He shows him the truth about himself. He uses the man's experiences, thoughts and emotional reactions merely as guiding posts on the roadway back to a new starting point. In this process, a re-education of the psyche takes place, a re-integration of the personality. He uncovers, one by one, the false assumptions of life, the misdirected emotions, the chaotic arrangement of thoughts, desires and impulses. He re-directs the stream of consciousness and the imprisoned thought from its bonds of fear, superstition and disappointment.

This, too, the spiritual practitioner does, but whereas the analytical method must uncover the entire emotional experience of the patient, in spiritual mind healing it is unnecessary for the practitioner or the patient to know just what caused the trouble. Wisdom, strength, courage and all harmonious conditions, are a direct result of spiritual power, *with which man is already equipped.* All power is from within, and as the deep within of the patient is awakened, weakness, fear and failure disappear. Loss is converted into gain and weakness into strength. The remedy for weakness is to develop power. Perfect love casts out fear and joy transmutes sadness into song.

Faith, through imagination has the power to heal. It can transmute depression into gladness. It can sublimate the energy of wrong emotional desire into constructive channels. Faith stirs at the roots of man's spiritual nature and quickens the flesh with its life giving message of love.

Both psychologist and metaphysician recognizes the value of faith as a healing and a regenerating power for good. *But faith must be in something deeper than the material self.* The patient must come to feel himself rooted in the Infinite.

Neither in psychological analysis nor in spiritual mind healing does the practitioner resort to mental influence or even to mental suggestion. It is a re-education of the inner mind, through understanding, that produces the cure. It is seeing, recognizing and accepting the truth about man's being that heals. The success of the procedure depends upon the patient seeing for himself that his fears are ungrounded, for just as Truth known becomes demonstrated, so fear, seen and understood, vanishes. There is no suggestion, hypnotism nor mental influence whatsoever in the process. It is self-knowing and self-seeing that produce the desired result.

If one carefully traces the evolution of the science of psychology, during the last one hundred years or so, he will find that starting with the experiments of Mesmer and others of his day, the method has entirely changed, and today could not be recognized as having the remotest relationship to its earlier form. The art has passed from mesmerism into hypnotism, from hypnotism into mental suggestion, and from mental suggestion into self-realization. Thus, in the long run, all psychological healing becomes self-healing through self-recognition; and this self-recognition is brought about through understanding. Superstition need play no part in the process, *but faith does, and always must, play a major role.*

Following the earlier experiments in mesmerism and hypnotism, a New England mechanic (perhaps one of the few original thinkers of history) discovered that he could sit with a patient, and, without resorting to any form of hypnotism, tell the patient exactly what was wrong with him. He read his soul, so to speak, using the same faculty that Jesus used when he told the woman at the well that she had been married five times and that the man she was now living with was not her husband.

From his experiments, our New England watchmaker, Phineas P. Quimby, discovered (and thus anticipated certain modern phases of psychology) that an explanation could produce a cure. He would explain to his patients that they were suffering from certain false thoughts, fears— later called phobias. He would explain away these fears. He said that his explanation was the cure. He was thought to be a quack, a charlatan, a fool, an atheist, but with a good-natured flexibility he evolved one of the most complete systems of spiritual philosophy the world has ever had. He called this the "Science of Being," or the "Science of Christ." In it, he laid bare what are today the essential elements of much of the new psychology. He was deeply spiritual and his work was filled with the thought of God. Today Jung tells us that *analysis without a restitution of faith cannot produce a permanent cure of a neurosis.*

Metaphysical or spiritual mind healing is based on the assumption that we live in a spiritual Universe NOW; that we are spiritual beings NOW; that the kingdom of heaven is at hand NOW; that the spiritual man is perfect NOW; that the Mind of God and the Energy of the Universe are available NOW.

The field of metaphysical deals with a Universal Wholeness more than does the field of psychology. Nor need this seem less scientific, for anything is scientific that produces results through known and demonstrable laws. The science of Mind is just as valid a science as is the science of psychology plus; for without denying the known laws of psychology, it becomes an extension of that field. It adds the Universal to the individual.

It proclaims the spiritual nature of man; it removes fear by introducing love. It places man in the Mind of God as some part of the Eternal Wholeness; it gives shelter to the soul; it satisfies the natural hunger of the intellect for the larger life. It surrenders indecision for Divine guidance; for human fear it gives spiritual faith. *This* to date, psychology has not done, for while the psychiatrist and the analyist may empty the soul, or the subjective, of its false impulses and desires, with what shall it re-fill this psychic void? This is its weakness.

If alcoholic addiction is an unconscious attempt to self-destruction; if it is a flight of fancy into an attempted oblivion, what would happen if the individual were to understand that there is no possible oblivion? What if he were to understand that the soul must be some part of God, sufficient unto itself in the great whole? If man is to be made whole in his own imagination, how will the desired result be obtained unless his wholeness is also linked with a Cosmic wholeness of which he is an important part? There seems no possible escape, and the newer psychology will, of necessity, have to wed itself to some form of religious emotion; not to superstition nor to a fear of God, but to a real fellowship with the Invisible. We come out of the Invisible. We live on, in and by It. How can we be separated from It?

The individual will be given back to himself only as he surrenders the lesser to the greater, for if "the libido" is really the "life urge," as it must be; and if the emotional desire toward self-expression is impulsed, because man's nature is a hidden reservoir of limitless possibilities, than what will stir the imagination toward fulfillment more than a conscious sense of one's unity with the "Oversoul"?

The psyche is that part of man's nature that lies between the Absolute and the relative. It is the repository of ideas, of ambitions, of hoes, longings and aspirations. It is the soul which lies open equally between Divine ideas and human forms. It is the creative center of man's life, or at least the avenue through which the creative urge works toward fulfillment. Ideas lodged in it seek self-expression The impulse in the psyche is spontaneous; its movement is mechanical, for we are dealing both with an engine and also with an engineer.

In our attempt to be scientific, let us not forget that there is a Scientist. In our attempt to know, let us not overlook the fact that to know implies a Knower; that that which is known, must be subject to that which knows. A lack of this perception is the fallacy of all materialism. But it need not be so, and today we see the hopeful sign of a new conception entering the field of research into the invisible nature of man. *God will have to be added, since His subtraction was in imagination alone.*

The metaphysician, or the spiritual mind practitioner, then, adds God to his psychology. He starts with the assumption that God is in all, over all, and through all. The impulse to express God is the very desire that lies back of the "libido." The emotional craving for self-expression is the "Father seeking such." That is, it is the natural and inevitable necessity that the Spirit become expressed through us.

If alcoholic addicts seek self-destruction through oblivion, it is because they have not been acquainted with themselves or their true relationship to the Universe in which they live. They have not known that there is an inner completeness, a spiritual wholeness, to their real natures. Surely it would not be amiss to tell them.

Why not add to the analysis of the soul, the healing power of the Spirit? Why not allow the imagination to enter into the larger life, not through a deep, inner conviction of man's spiritual nature? Spiritual experience is just as valid as any other experience. It need not be attended by any particular outward form of religious worship; no dogma has to attend it. All forms of superstition should carefully be avoided, for superstition itself is a flight of the imagination into a world of fantasy.

But just what would a spiritual re-education of the mind mean? It would mean, first of all, the removal of fear. Of what is man afraid? He is afraid of the universe in which he lives; he is afraid of what happens to him in this universe. He is afraid of pain, suffering, misunderstanding, of social and economic insecurity. He is hurt from his contacts with life. It matters not whether this fear started when he first entered a cold world, or whether it is a result of some form of frustration early in life... it is always FEAR.

There are a thousand and one forms of fear. Fear may be old, new or just beginning, but fear is always a feeling of some form of insecurity. Why not educate the mind into an understanding that the Divine Plan is perfect and that "good must come, at last, alike to all"? This has been the power of all religions. They may have been crude, superstitious and uncouth in many respects but, at least, they have been effective. Regeneration, transmutation, and sublimation through faith have been a reality in the experience of countless thousands throughout the ages. Nor has the human mind so far found any other power of sublimation that can equal faith and a constructive spiritual program. Why not make use of the highest and best in human experience? Why discard that which has proven effective wherever it has been used?

What is God but the Intelligent Life Principle running through everything, sustaining and animating everything? The very imagination through which man seeks his flight of fantasy (fleeing from Reality), could as easily have been directed into constructive channels for self-expression. Emerson felt the presence of the Invisible, peopling the lonely places with life, warmth and beauty. *This* is not a flight of fancy away from Reality, but rather the shadow of a rock in a weary place.

Where love is fear cannot linger, for love dissipates the anguish of fear as light neutralizes the darkness. The human sense of "aloneness" becomes submerged in the larger vision of an overshadowing Presence. Who could think that Jesus was laboring under a delusion when he stated that the Kingdom of Heaven is within?

To train one's mind to believe in this inner Kingdom is not illusion but the very essence of Reality. And as the analyst carefully replaces fear with confidence, in giving his patient back to himself, why not add the larger self, the greater hope, the deeper realization, the realization of the Self as an indestructible part of the Cosmos? Why not link this spiritual realization with the most trivial everyday occurrences, for the eternal day in which man is to live begins right here and now? To know of the immediate *now-ness* of the Kingdom, will produce, not a flight of fancy away from reality, but will have the reverse effect of causing the mind to enter into its inheritance now and here.

To feel a *Presence* guiding and directing, is not psychic confusion; it will *heal* psychic confusion. This form of Divine guidance is not to be confused with any belief in control by spirits. We must come to understand that *the* Spirit, Itself, is guiding, controlling and assisting. We must seek, consciously, to link our minds, not with *them*, but with It. No psychic confusion can follow such mental action.

Just as the analyst, gently and with deep understanding, leads his patient away from illusion and self-deception, so the spiritual mind practitioner must lead him into a new and better realization of his unity with the Cosmos. He points to spiritual truths, which the patient must practice for himself.

The spiritual practitioner, just as the psychologist, must be able to distinguish between true spiritual perception and psychic hallucination; between being guided by the Spirit and being influenced by alleged "spirits," for here is a field of tremendous illusion. As a matter of fact, the best psychologist is the one who includes in his technique that most subtle of all sciences—the science of common sense—but to this common sense should be added the elixir of true spiritual values!

One of the gravest errors into which spiritual mind healers have fallen is that of dogmatism, which has blinded them to the great good that might enter into their own field through an understanding of psychology. Truth is true wherever it may be found. An equally false position has been taken by many psychologists in their denial of spiritual values. The two fields should draw closer together if the world is to have the benefit of the best that is known today. *We must not forget that sugar is sweet whether we find it in a sugar bowl or dust pan.* This rather ordinary truth has been sadly overlooked by too many in both the field of metaphysics and of psychology.

Believing that there is "... one Mind common to all individual men," the spiritual mind practitioner realizes that no matter where his patient is, he may be reached and helped. This is a process whereby he thinks within himself for his patient. If asked to treat an alcoholic addict, the practitioner would turn back to his premise of perfect God, perfect man, perfect being. He would fill his own consciousness with the truth about Spirit, Its completion, Its satisfaction, Its wholeness. He would know that this same Spirit is the life of his patient! The patient must partake of the nature of Spirit. He would fill his own mind with the truth about the real Self of his patient; he would know that that Self was never depressed nor discouraged, that it was forever conscious of its unity with God, of its oneness with Spirit. The practitioner would use whatever argument he found necessary to bring his own mind to an acceptance of the truth about his patient. He would mentally free his patient from any belief that the habit of drink had any power over him. To the extent that he is able to recognize the complete freedom of his patient, this freedom will become objectified in the life of the addict—unless he willfully clings to his habit.

The practitioner must realize that the words he uses are the Law unto that thing whereto they are spoken. He must have a calm, unfaltering trust in his ability to reveal the *real* man, and in so doing, to free the physical man from the false belief. He must know that his patient is pure Spirit, and is wholly satisfied within himself. The discouragement, the maladjustment, the inhibitions never existed in Spirit, and can no longer appear to exist in or operate through the one whom he is healing.

Thus there comes to the addict a relief and a joyful expectancy that is not experienced when the psychologist merely stops with showing him what has brought about his present condition. He must be shown why he can reasonably expect freedom from this point on. This the spiritual mind practitioner gives. This we term psychology plus.

TREATMENT

Following is a suggested treatment for self-help. (If used for someone else, say "he is" instead of "I am.")

I know that the Spirit within me is God. I know that my life is God. I know that my mind and my imagination are filled with peace and with a sense of completeness. I am satisfied within myself. There is nothing that I fear or that I am afraid to meet. I am not running away from anything nor am I afraid of anything. Being whole and complete within myself, I need no stimulant to bolster my imagination and I seek no escape from reality. I am conscious of my ability to meet every situation in life with calmness and with peace. There is nothing in my memory that causes me to feel uncertain or unable to cope with any situation that can arise in my experience. The belief that I need alcohol in any form is an illusion. For I do not need anything outside myself to make me happy. I am happy and fulfilled now.

Within me is that which is perfect, that which is complete, that which is divine; that which was never born nor can die; that which lives, the eternal Reality. Within myself is peace, poise, power, wholeness and happiness. I need nothing outside myself to make me happy and contented. I fear nothing. I am whole and completely satisfied within myself. All the Power there is, and all the Presence there is, and all the Life there is, is God— the Living Spirit Almighty—and this Divine and Living Spirit is within me now. It is Wholeness. It is never weary. It is Life. It is complete Peace and cannot be afraid, nor can It seek to escape from anything—for It is All.

My life is never confused. It is always peaceful and happy. I know that my Divine Self is not separated from my physical and mental self. This consciousness of Wholeness, this recognition of my true Self, obliterates every belief that could cause me to wish for, or desire, any type of stimulant whatsoever. There is no memory of any such desire nor is there any expectation of any such desire. The truth about my real self reveals to my mind a complete freedom from any habit that could rob me of peace or of my rightful mentality.

Now, since there is no memory of ever having needed any false stimulant, and since there is no anticipation of ever needing to be bolstered up by anything but the Spirit, and since I know that I am Spirit, I know and realize my complete freedom, now and forever.

* * *

Editor's Note:

The preceding article has been written especially for those whose addiction is a definite escape mechanism. While this class of addicts is in the majority, of course it is also recognized that there are many other reasons for alcoholism. One having been healed of alcoholism, should be directed into some creative activity which gives him self-expression, the results of which compensate him for the apparent gratification he received through his addiction. It is generally accepted that some form of useful service to humanity, perhaps helping others who have suffered from the same delusions, is one of the best possible ways of seeking permanent happiness.

CPSIA information can be obtained
at www.ICGtesting.com
Printed in the USA
BVHW082017070922
646441BV00003B/512